NATIVE AMERICAN NATIONS

Cherokee

F.A. BIRD

Checkerboard Library

An Imprint of Abdo Publishing
abdobooks.com

ABDOBOOKS.COM

Published by Abdo Publishing, a division of ABDO, PO Box 398166, Minneapolis, Minnesota 55439.
Copyright © 2022 by Abdo Consulting Group, Inc. International copyrights reserved in all countries.
No part of this book may be reproduced in any form without written permission from the publisher.
Checkerboard Library™ is a trademark and logo of Abdo Publishing.

Printed in the United States of America, North Mankato, Minnesota
102021
012022

THIS BOOK CONTAINS RECYCLED MATERIALS

Design and Production: Mighty Media, Inc.
Editor: Liz Salzmann
Cover Photograph: Don Sniegowski/Flickr
Interior Photographs: Ad_hominem/Shutterstock Images, p. 7; Airman 1st Class Ryan J. Sonnier/US Air
    Force, p. 13; Alan Sharp/Flickr, p. 15; anthony heflin/Shutterstock Images, p. 5; Don Sniegowski/Flickr,
    p. 23; Jim Lane/Alamy Photo, p. 17; Joseph Sohm/Shutterstock Images, p. 11; Lehman and Duval/
    Wikimedia Commons, p. 27; Luc Novovitch/Alamy Photo, p. 19; PhotoTrippingAmerica/Shutterstock
    Images, p. 25; RodClementPhotography/Shutterstock Images, p. 9; Vineyard Perspective/
    Shutterstock Images, p. 29; Virginia State Parks staff/Wikimedia Commons, p. 21

Library of Congress Control Number: 2021943035

Publisher's Cataloging-in-Publication Data
Names: Bird, F.A., author.
Title: Cherokee / by F.A. Bird
Description: Minneapolis, Minnesota : Abdo Publishing, 2022 | Series: Native American nations | Includes
    online resources and index.
Identifiers: ISBN 9781532197161 (lib. bdg.) | ISBN 9781098219291 (ebook)
Subjects: LCSH: Cherokee Indians--Juvenile literature. | Indians of North America--Juvenile literature. |
    Indigenous peoples--Social life and customs--Juvenile literature. | Cultural anthropology--Juvenile
    literature.
Classification: DDC 973.0497--dc23

Contents

CHAPTER 1

Homelands

The Cherokee lived in the Appalachian Mountains for thousands of years. This area is in present-day Tennessee, Virginia, West Virginia, Kentucky, North Carolina, South Carolina, Georgia, and Alabama.

The Cherokee **homelands** had low mountains covered with forests. The forests were full of deer, turkey, bear, and other small game. The streams and rivers were full of fish.

The Cherokee call themselves *Anigaduwagi*. They watch over the earth and protect it.

The Appalachian Mountains are made up of several mountain ranges, including the Great Smoky Mountains.

CHAPTER 2

Society

The Cherokee lived in villages along streams and rivers. Often, each village had several hundred homes. It also had its own council and chiefs.

In the center of the village was a large, round council house and a public square. There, the Cherokee discussed important matters. The government was a **democracy**. It was based on people being equal.

The clan system is important to Cherokee society. There are seven Cherokee clans. They are the Wolf, Deer, Bird, Paint, Longhair, Blue, and Wild Potato. These clans connect the people to nature. They also make the Cherokee one large family.

Cherokee society was matrilineal. This means **ancestry** and kinship were traced through the mothers. Women were often the leaders and decision makers in traditional society.

THE CHEROKEE HOMELANDS

CHAPTER 3

Homes

During the summer, the Cherokee lived in large, rectangular houses. In winter they moved into smaller, round houses. These were easier to keep warm.

The type of construction the Cherokee used is called wattle and daub. Wattles are large mats woven out of sticks. These are attached to the house's frame. Daub is mud or clay that covers the wattle.

A round house had a thatched roof. A hole in its center let out the smoke from the firepit inside. There were benches along the wall that were used as sleeping platforms.

In the 1700s, European traders introduced metal tools to the Cherokee. Some Cherokee used the new tools to build log cabins instead of their traditional homes.

A Cherokee house

CHAPTER 4

Food

The Cherokee planted gardens with corn, squash, beans, potatoes, melons, and pumpkins. They also gathered berries, fruits, nuts, and herbs. The Cherokee hunted bear, turkey, and deer with bows and arrows. They hunted small animals, such as game birds, with blowguns.

Deer were important to the Cherokee. They used almost every part of the animal. The Cherokee ate the meat. They used the hides to make leather moccasins and clothes. They made tools, needles, and ornaments from the bones. The Cherokee fished with hooks carved from bone. They also caught fish with spears, bows and arrows, traps, and nets woven from plant fibers.

Traditional Cherokee teachings emphasized maintaining balance with the natural world. So, the Cherokee were careful not to kill more animals or plants than they needed to survive.

The Cherokee made blowguns from river cane. A blowgun was about six feet (1.8 m) long.

CHAPTER 5

Clothing

The Cherokee **homelands** had hot, sticky summers. So, the Cherokee wore little clothing. Men and boys wore only **breechcloths** and moccasins. Women and girls wore only skirts. Young children wore no clothes at all.

In the cold winters, men wore **buckskin** leggings and shirts. Women wore soft skirts and dresses made from deerskin and mulberry bark. Both men and women wore fur robes to keep warm. They also wore jewelry made of bone, shell, and beads.

After the Europeans arrived, the Cherokee traded for goods such as brass kettles, blankets, and cloth. One type of cloth they traded for was **calico**.

Cherokee women used calico to make dresses and skirts. Today, this style of dress has become known as a "tear dress." Many believe the name of the dress came from the way the women cut the cloth by tearing it. Men wrapped calico around their heads like turbans.

A man wearing traditional Cherokee clothing from the 1800s.

CHAPTER 6

Crafts

Cherokee men made **dugout** canoes. They carefully selected a tulip poplar tree with a large, straight trunk. The Cherokee said a prayer to thank the tree for giving up its life. Then, they set a small fire at the tree's base to help cut it down.

After the tree was down, the men removed the bark. Then they hollowed out the trunk with fire. Finally, they carved the outside of the trunk into a canoe shape. Making a canoe took much skill, work, and patience.

Cherokee women created baskets from river cane and white oak. Today, baskets are also made from honeysuckle. The baskets are usually made in round or rectangular shapes.

A Cherokee man makes a canoe at Oconaluftee Indian Village in North Carolina.

CHAPTER 7

Family

Cherokee marriage ceremonies were brief and simple. The bride and groom met at the council house. The groom gave the bride a venison ham. The bride gave the groom an ear of corn. After the offering of gifts, the ceremony continued with a great feast and dance.

The new couple lived with the wife's family. Her family included her mother, her married sisters and their families, and her unmarried brothers.

If the husband and the wife divorced, the woman and her children remained with the woman's family. The man returned to his mother's family. He lived there until he married again.

In Cherokee society, the children belong to the mother's clan. Clans are very important. Women and men cannot marry people from their own clan. This is because clan members are considered one family.

A Cherokee wedding ceremony

CHAPTER 8

Children

Boys learned to hunt and fish from their fathers and **uncles.** A strong friendship existed between them for their entire lives.

The most important men in a boy's life were his uncles. An uncle decided when the boy was old enough to go to war and help make family decisions.

The women taught Cherokee girls home and gardening skills. Cherokee children were never spanked. But the family elders teased them if they **misbehaved**.

Children perform a dance called the Ant Dance at a festival in North Carolina.

CHAPTER 9

Traditions

According to Cherokee tradition, the sky is made of solid rock. The earth is an island, which hangs from the sky by four ropes. The Cherokee descended from the first man, Kanati, and the first woman, Selu.

When Kanati needed food, he made arrows to hunt with. Then he went into the **woodlands** to a place where a giant rock stood. He pushed the rock to one side. Out from an underground cave came a deer or other game. He killed the animal instantly with one arrow.

Selu took a large basket into a building where the food was stored. Once inside, she rubbed her stomach, and the basket became nearly filled with corn. When she rubbed her legs, the basket filled the rest of the way with beans. Selu prepared the corn and beans to eat. The Cherokee believe this tradition is why Cherokee men became hunters, and Cherokee women tended the homes and gardens.

Cherokee gardens often include corn, sunflowers, and peppers.

CHAPTER 10

War

The Cherokee went to war to avenge the killing of relatives. The spirits of the dead family members could not rest until their families avenged the crime.

The entire village had to agree to go to war. War parties usually consisted of 20 to 40 men and one woman. She was called the war woman. She watched the **captives**, and she cooked for the entire party.

During war, the Cherokee men wore deer tails and white feathers in their hair. They did this so they could tell themselves apart from the enemy during battle. When the war party killed the same number of enemies as relatives who had been killed in their village, they went home.

Cherokee men performed dances before going to war and when negotiating peace with other nations.

CHAPTER 11

Contact with Europeans

The Cherokee first met Europeans in 1540. That's when Spanish explorer Hernando de Soto and his men reached the Cherokee **homelands** in South Carolina and Georgia.

Later, the Cherokee signed treaties with the British. The Cherokee and British fought the American colonists in the **American Revolution**.

In 1830, the US Congress passed the Indian Removal Act. This allowed the United States to move the Cherokee and other Native Americans off their traditional homelands so Europeans could settle in the area.

Native American men, women, and children were forced to walk to present-day Oklahoma. More than 4,000 Cherokee died during the journey. This 800-mile (1,287 km) march is known today as the Trail of Tears.

The Cherokee National Museum is in Tahlequah, Oklahoma. It celebrates Cherokee culture, and honors those who suffered on the Trail of Tears.

CHEROKEE NATIONAL MUSEUM

CHAPTER 12

Sequoyah

Sequoyah (Sik-wa-yi) was born around 1770. His mother was Cherokee. Her family came from a long line of chiefs. In 1809, Sequoyah heard that white men could read marks on paper. These marks carried the voices of men a great distance.

Sequoyah believed the Cherokee language could also be written. He listened to the sounds of the Cherokee language. Then he created a mark for each of the sounds. Sequoyah's Cherokee alphabet has 86 symbols. His first student was his six-year-old daughter. She learned to read and write the Cherokee language from her father's alphabet.

The alphabet was easy to learn. The Cherokee learned quickly. Soon, there was a Cherokee newspaper and books written in Cherokee. The National Cherokee Council gave Sequoyah a medal for his accomplishment.

Sequoyah

CHAPTER 13

The Cherokee Today

The Indian Removal Act and the Trail of Tears were **extremely harmful to the Cherokee people.** But even with such difficulties, the Cherokee and their **culture** has survived.

Some Cherokee were able to **reclaim** land in their traditional **homelands** in North Carolina. Some have made Oklahoma their new home. Other Cherokee people became scattered throughout the world. Many of them are now trying to find their way back to their Cherokee roots.

Today, there are three federally recognized Cherokee tribes. These are the Eastern Band of Cherokee Indians of North Carolina, the Cherokee Nation of Oklahoma, and the United Keetoowah Band of Cherokee Indians of Oklahoma.

Miss Cherokee contestants ride in the Cherokee National Homecoming parade in Tahlequah, Oklahoma.

Glossary

American Revolution—from 1775 to 1783. A war for independence between Great Britain and its North American colonies. The colonists won and created the United States of America.

ancestry—a line of descent.

breechcloth—a piece of cloth, usually worn by men. It wraps between the legs and around the waist.

buckskin—a soft leather made from the skin of a deer.

calico—a cotton fabric with a colorful pattern.

captive—someone who has been captured and held against their will.

culture—the customs, arts, and tools of a nation or a people at a certain time.

democracy—a governmental system in which the people vote on how to run their country.

dugout—a boat made by hollowing out a log.

homeland—the area where a particular group of people lives or comes from.

misbehave—to break a rule or behave badly.

reclaim—to get back something that was lost or taken away.

woodland—land covered with trees and bushes.

ONLINE RESOURCES

To learn more about the Cherokee, please visit **abdobooklinks.com** or scan this QR code. These links are routinely monitored and updated to provide the most current information available.

Index